What Is It?

This book belongs to

_____

What Is It?
A Language Learning Book for Wonderful Kids with Autism

PEC Books. ™
Twin Taurus Publishing ™

Published by PEC BOOKS ™ and Twin Taurus Publishing ™ of South Portland, Maine, USA.

PECBooks.com
TwinTaurusPublishing.com

ISBN (10) :   1614240000
ISBN(13) :   978-1-61424-000-6

Library of Congress Control Number: 2011941973

What Is It?

The ability to ask questions is a fundamental life skill. Asking questions not only enhances a child's learning potential, but is also critical to his or her safety and independence. Imagine living a single day without the capacity to identify objects in the world around you. "What is it?" is the first and most important question a child can ask.

This uniquely effective picture book is the cooperative effort of Parents, Experts, and Children (PEC). It is designed to teach wonderful kids with developmental delays like Autism Spectrum Disorders by minimizing learning interference elements and making use of the extraordinary gifts so many challenged children possess. Repeated readings help demonstrate the purpose of asking questions and encourage children to ask independently.

Books by
Parents, Experts, and Children

PEC Books are learning tools created by Parents, Experts, and Children. PEC projects reflect the experience, research, and wisdom of those most familiar with the challenges and opportunities that come with early childhood education and special needs. PEC Books are specifically designed for use with children facing developmental disabilities, but are beneficial to children of all abilities. Parents and educators can increase the effectiveness of this book by clearly demonstrating the use of questions in casual, real-life situations.

What is it?

It's a tree.

What is it?

It's a cupcake.

What are they?

They're balloons.

What is it?

It's a bike.

What are they?

They're birds.

What is it?

It's an airplane.

What are they?

They're jelly beans.

What is it?

It's a teddy bear.

What are they?

They're flowers.

What is it?

It's a dump truck.

What is it?

It's a truck.

What are they?

They're fish.

What are they?

They're blocks.

What are they?

They're crackers.

What is it?

It's an apple.

What is it?

It's a sailboat.

What is it?

It's a banana.

What is it?

It's a train.

A note of thanks...

To the parents, experts, and children who have contributed to this project both directly and indirectly, a tremendous debt of gratitude is owed. These books would not be possible without your interest, ideas, time, and effort.

To the heroic women and men who devote their lives and careers to the advancement of children with developmental challenges, no words could ever convey our appreciation. Your dedication and constant efforts make a very real difference in the fight to save children whose gifts might otherwise be overlooked and whose potential would likely be discarded. Thank you.

6927778R10023

Made in the USA
San Bernardino, CA
18 December 2013